SQUIRES KITCHEN'S GUIDE TO MAKING

more
iced flowers

First published in September 2013 by
B. Dutton Publishing Limited, The Grange,
Hones Yard, Farnham, Surrey, GU9 8BB.

Copyright: Ceri DD Griffiths 2013

ISBN-13: 978-1-905113-48-4

Publisher: Beverley Dutton
Group Editor: Jenny Stewart
Editor: Jenny Royle
Editorial Assistant: Frankie New
Editorial & Advertising Assistant: Adele Duthie
Art Director/Designer: Sarah Ryan
Designer: Zena Deakin
Graphic Designer & Photography Stylist: Louise Pepé
Graphic Designer: Abbie Johnston
Photography: Alister Thorpe
Printed in China
Wallpapers supplied by wallpaperdirect.co.uk

Disclaimer

The Author and Publisher have made every effort to
ensure that the contents of this book, if followed carefully,
will not cause harm or injury or pose any danger. Please
note that some inedible items, such as flower stamens
and cake dowels, have been used in the projects in this
book. All such inedible items must be removed before the
cake is eaten. Similarly, any non food-grade equipment
and substances, such as non-toxic glue, must not come
into contact with any cake or cake covering that is to be
eaten. Neither the Author nor the Publisher can be held
responsible for errors or omissions and cannot accept
liability for injury, damage or loss to persons or property,
however it may arise, as a result of acting upon guidelines
and information printed in this book.

SQUIRES KITCHEN'S GUIDE TO MAKING

more iced flowers

Ceri DD Griffiths

Decorative piped sugar flowers for cakes, cookies and desserts

acknowledgements

A huge thank you goes to my mother and sister for their support; Stef, Rachel and Lucy for their friendship; Jane Creed for her honest feedback; and Barry Dickinson and Gail Hyatt for their generosity in sharing knowledge and expertise. Last and by no means least, thanks to all of the team at B. Dutton Publishing and Squires Kitchen for allowing me to explore my love of cake artistry.

introduction

I graduated as a Master Baker and Confectioner in 1980 from Cardiff College of Food Technology and Science. In the following years I worked in the bakery industry both in the UK and abroad and this was where the seeds of my own style were nurtured.

After so much positive feedback from the release of my first book, *Squires Kitchen's Guide to Making Iced Flowers*, a second publication was an obvious choice. It was a decision that I was more than pleased about as I had so many more flowers that I wanted to share. When I started to plan this second book, I wanted to continue to offer exciting projects with a contemporary twist. You won't find a single royal iced cake between the covers of this book and that is intentional. I fully believe that the way forward for royal icing is the contemporary world of multi-medium cakes.

This book contains iced flowers for both the beginner and advanced sugarcrafter; I hope these skills become the first steps on a path that will lead you to the same love affair I have with royal icing.

I am often heard to say, "You learn more when you laugh and less when you stress," so have fun with it. It's only icing – you can always eat your mistakes along the way!

contents

essential equipment and edibles

When creating iced flowers, it is important to have everything you need to hand before you begin. Due to the speed at which royal icing dries, you do not have the luxury of time that you have when creating sugarpaste flowers. Before you start, make sure that you go through all the stages for creating the flower you wish to produce and take note of the edibles and equipment you will need. By doing so you will be able to make sure you have all the materials and equipment ready before you start. Having everything prepared means that you will be able to relax and enjoy creating your iced flowers.

Below is the basic equipment you will need for making the iced flowers in this book.

equipment for making iced flowers

1 Bowls suitable for storing royal icing

2 Card, acetate or food-safe plastic for making stencils

3 Cling film

4 Cocktail sticks

5 Craft knife

6 Dimpled foam

7 Dusting brush

8 Flat flower nail

9 Food mixer strong enough to make royal icing (not pictured)

10 Glaze Cleaner (SK)

11 Kitchen foil

12 Lily nail: I have used Wilton, set of four: ½", 1¼", 1⅝", 2¼"

13 Non-stick board

14 Nozzle adaptor (optional)

15 Palette knife

16 Parchment, silicone, nylon or plastic piping bags

17 Piping nozzles: I have used PME Supertubes nos. 1, 1.5, 2, 3, 4, 42, 50, 51, 52, 56, 57S, and Wilton 81, 103, 104 in this book

18 Small paintbrush

19 Small paint palette for mixing colours

20 Small pointed scissors

21 Spatula

22 Stamens

23 Polystyrene block

24 Tea towel

25 Tweezers

26 Wax paper or cellophane

parts of a petal nozzle

All instructions given within this book are for right-handed pipers, however piping in the opposite direction (for left-handed pipers) will achieve the same flower.

It is important to note that there are three basic types of petal nozzles available and they are marked R, L, or S. Nozzles marked with an R are for right-handed pipers, those marked with an L are for left-handed pipers and those marked with an S are straight and therefore suitable for all pipers. Some brands have no markings at all so check with your supplier before you buy.

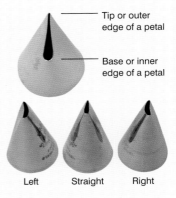

Tip or outer edge of a petal

Base or inner edge of a petal

Left   Straight   Right

Although iced flowers do not require too many different edible materials, there are a few essentials that you will always need. Any specific requirements are given at the beginning of each project.

edibles

1 Confectioners' Glaze (SK)
2 Cornflour
3 Dust Food Colours (SK)
4 Edible Glue (SK)
5 Glycerine
6 Instant Mix Royal Icing (SK)
7 Liquid Food Colours (SK)
8 Metallic Dust Food Colours (SK)
9 Pollen-style Food Colours (SK)
10 Sugar Florist Paste, SFP (gum paste) (SK)
11 White vegetable fat

tutor tip

If you choose to dust your royal iced flowers when they are dry, it is best to dust them prior to arranging them on your cake. Do not dust your flowers if you want to store them for later use, as the colour may fade over time.

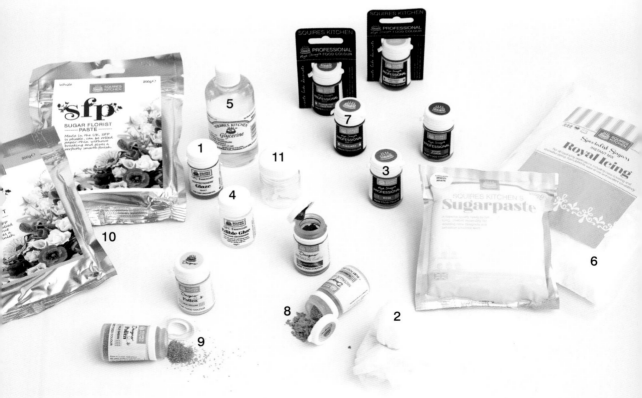

working with royal icing

how to make royal icing

I used Squires Kitchen's Instant Mix Royal Icing for all the flowers and projects in this book. The advantage of using a pre-mix is that, if you follow the instructions on the packet, your royal icing will be the right consistency every time. Always sieve any pre-mix thoroughly prior to use to distribute the ingredients evenly as this will help you to achieve the same consistency each time.

If you would like to make your own royal icing, you can follow this basic recipe.

edibles

455g (1lb) icing sugar
15g (½oz) SK Fortified Albumen powder
Cooled, boiled water

equipment

Small bowl
Weighing scales
Sieve
Mixer
Spatula

Makes 455g (1lb) royal icing

1 Reconstitute the albumen powder as per the instructions on the pack.

2 Weigh and sieve the icing sugar.

3 Place ¾ of the icing sugar into the mixing bowl, lower the K beater into it and switch the mixer on at a slow speed. Add ¾ of the reconstituted albumen.

4 As the royal icing mixes, check the consistency: if it appears to be thick and syrupy then add a little more icing sugar; if it appears to be dry and crumbly, add a little more reconstituted albumen.

5 Periodically stop the mixer and scrape down the inside and bottom of the mixing bowl with a spatula so that there are no pockets of unmixed icing sugar.

Run-out icing

Soft-peak icing

Firm-peak icing

6 Once the royal icing is approximately the right consistency (i.e. similar to a thick cake batter) increase the speed on the mixer. After a few minutes the icing will become whiter in colour and fluffier in texture.

7 When the royal icing is white and fluffy, take it off the mixer and beat it by hand as this will help you judge its consistency. Achieving the correct consistency of royal icing will come with practice, however you are aiming to mix the icing so that it holds a firm peak when you lift away from the icing with a palette knife. At this point you can adjust the consistency for the project you are working on by adding more reconstituted albumen or sieved icing sugar.

storing royal icing

1 When you've finished working with your bowl of royal icing, scrape the sides of the bowl down and smooth the icing to a flat surface.

2 Using a clean, damp cloth wipe the insides of the bowl. This is important because if there is any icing on the sides of the bowl and it crusts over, it can drop into your royal icing and block piping nozzles when you are piping.

3 Place a piece of cling film directly onto the surface of the royal icing. Make sure there are no air pockets and that the cling film is also in contact with the inside of the bowl.

4 Lay a clean, damp cloth or tea towel over the top of the bowl and set aside.

5 When you use royal icing after storage you do not need to re-mix it in a machine; beating it by hand using a spatula will be enough to re-establish the consistency of the royal icing.

Storing royal icing varies depending upon the climate you live in. I don't need to store my royal icing in a fridge, but it is essential if you live in a hotter climate. If you do have to refrigerate your royal icing, always let it come back up to room temperature before you use it.

Personally, I don't keep my royal icing for more than three days as I like to use it fresh. However, as a general guideline, I would not recommend keeping royal icing for more than five days as after this time the structure begins to weaken and the egg albumen may go off.

using colour with royal icing

Colour is a wonderful element when designing cakes and its clever use will set your creations above all others, adding that elusive 'wow' factor.

If you are making a cake for someone you know or as a commission, the colours you use will normally be dictated by the client; however, a basic knowledge of colour balance is essential for pleasing – and in some cases, dramatic – effects in cake design. One of the best pieces of equipment for use in cake design is an artist's colour wheel: this small, readily available reference guide will show at a glance how monochromatic, complementary and contrasting colours in different shades and tones can enhance the overall impact of your design.

When colouring royal icing, only liquid or dust food

colours are generally recommended. Paste food colours that contain glycerine (also known as glycerol) and glycerides should be avoided for royal icing as they will prevent the icing from fully drying. However, it is worth noting that all paste food colours in the Squires Kitchen range do not contain glycerine and are suitable for use with royal icing.

Liquid food colour is perfect for pastel or normal colouration, however for deep colours such as red, black, deep purple and royal blue the use of dust (powder) food colour is essential. Adding too much liquid colour will change the consistency of the icing, making it too fluid to work with. When using dust food colours it is best to colour a small portion of royal icing as it will take a lot of dust food colour to get the intensity of a strong colour. Making intensely coloured royal icing 24 hours prior to its use will prevent the appearance

of spots on your wet royal icing caused by the particles of dust colour dissolving at different rates. I would recommend only using intensely coloured royal icing for accent pieces and line work, rather than for more prominent features on a cake. There is the possibility these colours will bleed into surrounding paler colours over time, so these accents should be added to your creation last.

One final note on the use of colour on cakes: colour can be very significant for the recipient of the cake. If you are making cakes for sale or for someone you don't know directly, always ask questions concerning colours and their meaning at the consultation stage of cake designing, before you start work on the cake. Colours can also evoke emotions and preconceived imagery so it is wise to be aware of these when designing a cake for a specific event. The following are a few examples of meanings associated with colours:

Blue – calmness, dignity

Black – elegance, rebellion

Green – freshness, naturalness

Purple – royalty, sophistication

Red – excitement, danger

White – purity, kindness

Yellow – joy, reminiscence

using a piping bag

Once you have made and coloured the royal icing as required, you will need to use it in a piping bag (unless you are making stencilled flowers such as the forget-me-not or water lily). To use a piping bag:

1 If you are using a parchment paper bag, snip off approximately 1.3cm (½") from the tip. Place the required piping nozzle into a piping bag so that the tip of the nozzle protrudes from the end.

2 Hold the bag in one hand and use a palette knife to ²/₃ fill the bag with royal icing.

3 Fold the top of the bag over away from the seam, then fold the corners in (like an envelope) to seal the top of the bag and push the icing to the end to expel any air.

4 Hold the bag near the folded end and squeeze with your thumb and index finger until the icing comes out of the nozzle. Support the bag with your other hand as you pipe.

top tips on royal icing

- Use freshly made royal icing whenever possible, as this will give you better results when making iced flowers.

- Always keep the end of your piping nozzle clean as this will make it easier to control when piping.

- When using royal icing, your best friend is a slightly damp, fine-tipped paintbrush as you can use it to reposition icing without having to re-pipe the decoration.

- By filling a piping bag with two similar colours of royal icing, you will be able to create unique two-toned flowers which will not need dusting (see page 73).

- When dusting royal icing with food colour, the fine blending of colour can only be achieved if you are using a dust colour fractionally lighter or darker than the iced flower you are working on.

- With iced flowers, always remember the phrase 'less is more'. Do not colour up a large batch of royal icing for flowers as a little goes a long way.

- Do not worry about trying to match the colour of subsequent batches of royal icing to your original icing colour. As long as you are using the same food colour, any variations will only add interest to your finished flowers, giving them a more natural-looking colour range.

- If you don't need to make up a whole bag of SK Instant Mix Royal Icing, simply weigh out as much as you need. Make sure you sieve the mixture at least twice before weighing it out and adding the required amount of cooled, boiled water and mixing. Seal the open bag.

- When creating stencilled flowers, if you find that your card or plastic stencils are too thin, stick two layers together to double the thickness.

covering a cake

Before you decorate a celebration cake you will need to coat it, either with royal icing or sugarpaste (rolled fondant). If you are using a rich fruit cake it should be covered with marzipan first, then either sugarpaste or royal icing: I have described the sugarpaste covering method below as this was used for all of the cake projects in this book. Sponge cakes are usually crumb-coated with a thin layer of buttercream or ganache, then coated with sugarpaste (this is much quicker than coating with royal icing).

Once your cake is covered it is ready to be decorated with beautiful iced flowers or any other decoration of your choice.

how to sugarpaste a rich fruit cake

edibles

Square or round rich fruit cake

Apricot jam

SK Marzipan

SK Sugarpaste (rolled fondant)

Icing sugar in a shaker

equipment

Sieve

Large, serrated knife

Non-stick board

Rolling pin

Marzipan spacers (optional)

Thin cake board (larger than your cake)

Square or round cake drum (appropriate shape and size for your cake)

Silicone pastry brush

Small sharp knife or pizza wheel

Smoothers

Spirit level (optional)

1 Sieve the apricot jam then boil it to make a glaze (this destroys any bacteria present). Prepare the fruit cake by levelling it with a large, serrated knife.

2 Dust a work surface or a non-stick board with sieved icing sugar to prevent sticking and knead the marzipan to soften it. Roll out the marzipan to a thickness of approximately 7mm (¼"), ensuring that it is large enough to cover the top of the cake. If you have marzipan spacers, use these to help achieve a uniform depth. Once rolled out, lay the marzipan over a thin cake board.

 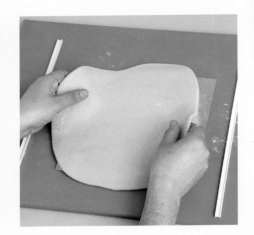

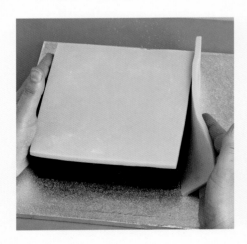 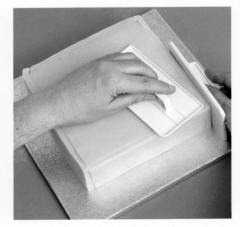

3 Turn the fruit cake over so that the base of the cake now becomes the top, then use a silicone pastry brush to brush the top of the cake with warm apricot glaze. Carefully turn the cake over onto the marzipan so that the apricot glaze sticks to the marzipan. Use a sharp knife to trim any excess marzipan from around the top of the cake.

4 Place the cake drum onto the cake so that the fruit cake is sandwiched between the cake drum and the thin cake board. Hold the cake carefully between the drum and the cake board, then turn the cake up the right way and lift off the thin cake board. Adjust the cake on the drum so that it sits squarely in the centre. If there is a small gap between the cake and the cake drum, roll a thin sausage of marzipan and use it to fill the gap before covering the sides.

5 Dust a work surface with sieved icing sugar and roll out a strip of marzipan to approximately 7mm (¼") thick. For a square cake, use a small sharp knife or pizza wheel to cut the marzipan so it is slightly larger than one side of the cake. Brush one side of the cake with warm apricot glaze, then attach the marzipan strip and use a sharp knife to trim away any excess. Repeat for each side of the cake. For best results, marzipan the opposite sides of the cake then coat the remaining uncovered sides. This method will ensure you do not distort the overall shape of the cake. For a round cake, cut a long strip to go all the way around the cake, brush the cake sides with warm apricot glaze and wrap the marzipan around the cake. Trim neatly at the join and smooth with a cake smoother.

6 Make sure that the marzipan is stuck to the cake and use smoothers for a polished finish. Use the palm of your hand to gently smooth out and soften any sharp corners or edges.

7 Roll out the sugarpaste to a thickness of approximately 7mm (¼") ensuring that it is large enough to cover the top and sides of the cake in one go. Coat the cake with one piece of sugarpaste, working from the centre of the cake outwards to the edges and down the sides, smoothing as you go. Should an air pocket appear, use a sterilised pin to pierce it. Use sugarpaste smoothers to obtain a smooth, polished finish and trim neatly around the base with a sharp knife.

tutor tips

This method will give the cake a slightly sharper top edge than covering all-in-one with marzipan but will still allow you to coat the cake with one piece of sugarpaste.

It is a good idea to use a small spirit level to ensure that the top of your cake is level as this will prevent problems later on. Before you check your cake, make sure your work surface is also level.

how to sugarpaste a sponge cake

edibles

Round or square sponge cake

Buttercream or ganache

Jam (optional)

Icing sugar in a shaker

SK Sugarpaste (rolled fondant)

equipment

Round or square cake drum (appropriate shape and size for your cake)

Thin cake board (same shape and size as the cake)

Palette knife

Large, serrated knife

Rolling pin

Side scraper (optional)

Smoothers

Small sharp knife or pizza wheel

1 Prepare the sponge cake by levelling it with a large serrated knife, then layering and filling it with buttercream or ganache and jam if desired. Secure the cake to the cake board with a little buttercream to make it easier to handle whilst you are covering it. Coat the whole cake with a thin layer of buttercream or ganache to secure any loose crumbs to the cake. Place the cake in the refrigerator for 15–20 minutes to chill before covering it with sugarpaste.

2 Weigh the required amount of sugarpaste (see project instructions) and knead well until it becomes soft, pliable and crack free. Place the softened sugarpaste in a food-grade plastic bag to prevent it from drying out.

3 Lightly dust the work surface with icing sugar and roll out the sugarpaste to approximately 3–5mm (approximately 1/8") in depth, aiming to keep a square or circular shape. Keep turning the paste while you are rolling it out to prevent it from sticking, and dust the board with a little more icing sugar if necessary. To work out how big the diameter of the sugarpaste needs to be to cover the cake all in one go, multiply the height of the cake by two and then add this to the width of the cake. For example, to cover a 15cm (6") round cake which is 7.5cm (3") tall, you will require a circle of sugarpaste that is 30.5cm (12") in diameter.

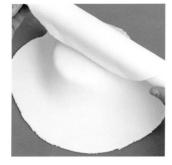

4 Use a rolling pin to lift the piece of sugarpaste and drape it centrally over the cake. Place the rolling pin to one side and immediately smooth out any air bubbles from the top with the palm of your hand. Run your palm around the top edge to secure the paste in position. For best results, work your way around the cake with your palms, smoothing the sugarpaste evenly as you go to prevent pleats forming. If you start to get folds at the base of the cake, gently pull the sugarpaste away from the side of the cake and carefully smooth it back into place with your fingers.

5 Once you have completely covered the cake with sugarpaste all the way to the bottom of the cake board, use a sharp knife or a pizza wheel to trim off the excess. As the cake is on a thin cake board, you can easily lift it up to trim any excess paste from the bottom without damaging the cake.

6 Smear a little buttercream or ganache in the centre of the cake drum and place the coated cake, still on its thin board, onto the drum. Use smoothers to polish the surface of the sugarpaste for a smooth finish. If you find any air pockets under the paste, carefully pierce them with a sterilised pin. To finish, cover the cake drum with a strip of sugarpaste and then use a small, sharp knife to trim it neatly at the edge of the cake drum.

tutor tip

You are less likely to tear or overstretch the sugarpaste if you smooth the paste in an upward direction.

recipes

No-Bake Chocolate Christmas Puddings

ingredients

150g (5¼oz) sultanas (golden, if available)

50g (1¾oz) dried apricots (finely chopped)

1tsp ground cinnamon

1tsp ground nutmeg

1tsp ground allspice

2tbsp brandy, or alcohol of your choice

100g (3½oz) SK Belgian Milk Chocolate Couverture

100g (3½oz) SK Belgian Dark Chocolate Couverture

50g (1¾oz) unsalted butter

4tbsp golden syrup

equipment

Small bowl

Heatproof bowl

Saucepan

Plastic spatula

Silikomart medium (50mm) half-sphere silicone mould or silicone mould of your choice

Preparation time: approx. 3 hours

Makes approx. 8 small half-sphere puddings

1 Place all of the fruit and spices into a small bowl with the alcohol and leave to soak for 30 minutes, stirring occasionally.

2 Place both dark and milk chocolate couvertures, unsalted butter and golden syrup into a heatproof bowl. Sit this bowl over a saucepan of simmering water, making sure that the water doesn't quite touch the bowl. Gently stir the contents until all have melted and the mixture is a rich, silky consistency. Be careful not to get any water into the chocolate as it will thicken it and cause it to 'seize'.

3 Add the fruit to the melted chocolate mixture and gently stir until all of the fruit is incorporated and evenly distributed.

4 Spoon the mixture into the half-sphere silicone moulds and gently tap the mould so that the chocolate works its way down to the very bottom, filling any air pockets.

5 Place the moulds into the refrigerator for approximately two hours prior to serving. Silicone moulds make it easy to release the puddings and they will give a glossy finish to the chocolate.

These sugar cookies are simple to make and have a delicious hint of orange. For different flavour variations, try substituting the orange zest for lemon or grapefruit zest.

Orange Sugar Cookies

ingredients

285g (10oz) plain (all-purpose) flour

1tsp baking powder

115g (4oz) caster sugar

90g (3oz) unsalted butter

1tbsp golden syrup

1 egg (medium or large), lightly beaten

1tsp vanilla extract

½tsp orange extract (optional if using a small orange)

Zest of 1 medium orange

equipment

Sieve

Mixing bowl

Food-grade plastic bag or cling film

65mm (2½") round fluted cutter, or other cutter of your choice

Makes approx. 35 round cookies

tutor tip

If you want to make all your cookies the same depth, use a pair of rounded ice lolly sticks or barbecue skewers as spacers.

1 Preheat the oven to 170°C/325°F/gas mark 3; if you have a fan-assisted oven you may have to adjust the baking time slightly.

2 Sieve the flour, baking powder and caster sugar into a mixing bowl. Rub the butter through the dry ingredients until you achieve a fine crumb.

3 Make a well in the centre of the mixture and add all of the remaining ingredients. Use your hands to combine all of the ingredients into a ball of dough. The dough will appear to be very dry at first, but continue to knead well to achieve the desired consistency. Do not be tempted to add more liquid.

4 Wrap the cookie dough in cling film or seal it in a food-grade plastic bag and leave it in the refrigerator for approximately 20 minutes to allow it to mature. This dough can be left overnight should you wish to make the cookies the following day.

5 Dust a clean work surface with flour, remove the cookie dough from the refrigerator and roll out the cookie dough to a depth of approximately 3mm (¹/₈"). Cut out the cookies with a fluted cutter, place them on a baking sheet and immediately place them in the preheated oven.

6 Bake for 15–20 minutes or until they start to colour around the edges. Once your cookies have just started to take on colour, remove them from the oven and allow to rest for a couple of minutes before transferring to a cooling rack.

gerberas

edibles

SK Instant Mix Royal Icing

SK Professional Liquid Food Colours
of your choice

equipment

Piping bags

Piping nozzles: nos. 2, 50 (PME),
104 (Wilton)

Small palette knife

Wax paper

Flower nail

Round paintbrush (SK)

1   Make up some firm-peak royal icing and colour it with the liquid food colour of your choice. Fit a piping bag with a no. 104 petal nozzle, then fill the bag ²/₃ full with the coloured royal icing.

2   Attach a circle of wax paper to the head of a flower nail with a touch of royal icing.

3   To pipe the gerbera, hold the bag with the petal nozzle in the opposite direction to normal, so that the base (the widest part) of the nozzle will create the outside edge of the teardrop-shaped petal. Hold the flower nail between your thumb and index finger, pipe a long teardrop to create an individual petal and ensure that it finishes in the centre of the nail. Continue to pipe petals from the outside edge to the same central point, keeping the outside edge of the gerbera circular.

4   Pipe as many petals as required to complete the gerbera head, then use a slightly damp, round paintbrush to make sure all the petals meet in the middle. Once all the petals are piped, use the paintbrush to remove a circle of wet royal icing from the very middle of the gerbera to give you space to pipe the centre.

5   Colour a small amount of soft-peak royal icing so that it contrasts with the first colour. Fit a piping bag with a no. 2 nozzle and fill it ²/₃ full with the coloured royal icing. Pipe small peaks in concentric circles in the centre of the gerbera: aim to make a perfect circle.

6   For the tiny inner petals, colour a small amount of soft-peak royal icing in a third colour or a shade darker than the petal colour. Fit a piping bag with a no. 50 nozzle, fill it $2/3$ full with the coloured royal icing and pipe a row of tiny petals around the flower centre. Lift the wax paper with the gerbera off the flower nail and set it aside to allow the flower to dry. You should be able to remove the wax paper and attach the flower to the cake within 24 hours.

tutor tips

When making or piping flowers, it is a good idea to have one in front of you as a reference to help you make them appear realistic – the internet is a great resource for images of flowers.

If you prefer, you can attach a flower centre moulded from modelling paste to the gerbera instead of piping the centre. See instructions on page 32 for how to do this.

colourful cookie pops

Bright and bold, a fun display of these colourful gerbera cookie pops would look great on any party table.

edibles

Orange sugar cookies, see recipe on page 25

SK Instant Mix Royal Icing, approximately 15g (½oz) per cookie

SK Professional Liquid Food Colours of your choice

SK Mexican Modelling Paste (MMP) in the colour of your choice, approximately 20g (¾oz) per cookie

SK Piping Gel (optional)

White vegetable fat

SK Glycerine (optional)

equipment

Fluted round cutter: 65mm (2½")

Cookie sticks (optional)

Piping bags

Piping nozzles: nos. 50 (PME), 104 (Wilton)

Small palette knife

SK Great Impressions Petal Veiner Daisy Centres Mould (Set of 3)

Round paintbrush (SK)

Small round cutter: 2cm (¾")

1 Make the orange sugar cookie dough following the recipe on page 25. Cut out the cookies with a 65mm (2½") round fluted cutter and if you desire, insert an ovenproof cookie stick into each one before baking to make cookie pops. Allow to cool completely before decorating.

2 Colour some firm-peak royal icing with the liquid colour of your choice. Fit a piping bag with a no. 104 petal nozzle, then fill the bag ²/₃ full with the coloured icing.

3 Turn the cookie over so that the flatter side of the cookie is the side onto which you will pipe the flower. If you wish at this stage, you can cover the cookie with a disc of MMP cut from the same fluted circle cutter as the cookies. Attach it to the cookie with a little piping gel.

4 Rest the cookie on a flat surface and hold it firmly between your thumb and index finger. Following the instructions on pages 29 to 30, pipe gerbera petals onto the cookie. Once all the petals are piped, do not remove a circle of wet royal icing from the middle of the flower as this icing will stick the moulded flower centre in place.

5 To make the centre for the flower, choose the appropriate daisy centre mould for the size of the gerbera and grease your hands with a little white vegetable fat. Roll a small ball of MMP in a colour that complements the gerbera petals and press it firmly into the mould. Gently ease the shape out of the mould and use a 2cm (¾") round cutter to ensure the centre is perfectly round. Place the paste carefully onto the wet royal icing in the centre of the gerbera and leave to dry for around 2 hours. The centres can be made ahead of time if needed.

6 For the tiny inner petals, colour a small amount of soft-peak royal icing with the liquid colour of your choice. Fit a piping bag with a no. 50 nozzle and fill it ²/₃ full with the coloured royal icing, then pipe a row of tiny petals around the centre. Leave the icing to dry for 24 hours before you handle the decorated cookies.

tutor tips

To make the royal icing softer and easier to eat for cookies and cupcakes, add 1 teaspoon of glycerine to every 500g (1lb 1¾oz) of royal icing.

To top cupcakes with gerberas you can also pipe them in coloured buttercream instead of royal icing and use sweets to make the centres for treats that children will love.

It is a good idea to turn the cookie over before piping, as the flatter surface on the back of the cookies will make it easier to pipe the flower.

sunflowers

edibles

SK Instant Mix Royal Icing

SK Professional Liquid Food Colours:
Bulrush (Dark Brown), Sunflower

equipment

Piping bags

Piping nozzles: nos. 2, 52 (PME)

Small palette knife

Wax paper

Scissors

Pencil

Large flower nail

Small bowls

1 Firstly, decide how big you want the finished sunflower to be, then cut a circle of wax paper slightly larger than this. On the back of the wax paper, draw a circle in the centre with a pencil approximately ¼ the size of the outer circle. This circle will represent the centre of the sunflower; use the outer edge of the wax paper as a guide for where the petals should finish.

2 Turn the wax paper over so that the pencil markings are face down to avoid contact with the royal icing. Attach the wax paper to a large flower nail with a dab of royal icing.

3 Colour some soft-peak royal icing with Bulrush liquid food colour, fit a piping bag with a no. 2 nozzle and fill it ⅔ full with the coloured royal icing. Starting at the outer edge of the central circle, pipe concentric circles of dots in the centre until it is covered.

4 Make up some firm-peak royal icing, divide it into two bowls and colour the icing two different shades of yellow using different amounts of Sunflower liquid colour. Fit a piping bag with a no. 52 nozzle and place the darker yellow royal icing down one side of the bag and the paler

yellow icing down the other side. When you pipe, the royal icing should be two-toned.

5 The petals of the sunflower are piped like elongated leaves: start with the nozzle touching the centre of the flower and then gently draw the petal out whilst applying pressure to the piping bag. Once you reach the desired length, stop squeezing and gently pull away to create the point of the petal. Continue to pipe petals around the sunflower centre, making sure that they all join the centre. Once you have completed one circle of petals, pipe another set that overlaps the joins of the first petals.

6 Lift the wax paper with the sunflower off the flower nail and set it aside to dry on a flat surface. Leave this to dry for approximately 24 hours before removing from the wax paper.

summer days

edibles

12 cupcakes baked in SK Polka Dot Cupcake Cases: Cocktail Collection

100g (3½oz) buttercream, or more if you are also filling your cupcakes

SK Sugarpaste: Bridal White, approximately 20g (¾oz) per cupcake

SK Instant Mix Royal Icing, approximately 20g (¾oz) per cupcake

SK Professional Liquid Food Colour: Sunflower

SK Professional Paste Food Colours: Bulrush (Dark Brown), Leaf Green

SK Glycerine

SK Edible Glue

Icing sugar in a shaker

equipment

Piping bags

Piping nozzle: no. 52 (PME)

Round cutter: same size as the top of the cupcakes

Rolling pin

Small palette knife

Fine mesh sieve or small, sharp knife

1 Spread a thin layer of buttercream over the top of each cupcake. Lightly dust a work surface with icing sugar, colour the white sugarpaste with Leaf Green food colour, then roll out the paste thinly. Cut out 12 circles of paste with a round cutter and attach one to the top of each cupcake.

2 Colour a small amount of sugarpaste with Bulrush paste food colour and then roll it into a ball that is slightly smaller than the centre of the sunflower. Gently push the paste into the mesh of a sieve to give it a latticed pattern. If you prefer, you can achieve the same effect by marking lines onto a circle of paste with a small, sharp knife. Stick the disc of paste in the centre of the cupcake with a little edible glue.

3 Make up some firm-peak royal icing and add 1 teaspoon of glycerine for every 500g (1lb 1¾oz) of royal icing. Colour the royal icing as required and pipe the sunflower directly onto the sugarpaste following the instructions on pages 35 to 36.

tutor tips

Adding glycerine to royal icing will make it softer and easier to eat, which is ideal for cupcakes and cookies.

Use a large chocolate button as the centre of the flower to make these a particular favourite with children.

Give these vibrant sunflower cupcakes as gifts and they are guaranteed to make your friends and family smile.

morning glory

edibles

SK Instant Mix Royal Icing

SK Professional Liquid Food Colours:
Bluebell (Navy Blue), Daffodil (Yellow),
Leaf Green, Wisteria

White vegetable fat

equipment

Silicone piping bags

Piping nozzles: nos. 1.5, 42, 51 (PME);
2 x 103 (Wilton)

Small palette knife

Kitchen foil

Lily nail: 3cm (1¹/₈") (Wilton)

Round paintbrush (SK)

Scissors

Dimpled foam or cupped former

1 Fit two separate piping bags each with a no. 103 petal nozzle. Colour some firm-peak royal icing with Bluebell and Wisteria liquid colours to achieve the desired shade of blue and fill one piping bag ²/₃ full with blue royal icing. Make up some soft-peak icing and fill the other bag ²/₃ full with white royal icing.

2 Cut a small square of kitchen foil and lightly smear the shiny side with white vegetable fat. Push the foil into the lily nail with the shiny side facing upwards. Wrap the edge of the foil over the lip of the nail to keep it in place whilst piping.

3 To start the flower, pipe a ribbon of white royal icing around the inside of the base of the lily nail; the widest part of the nozzle will make the bottom of the flower.

4 Use the blue royal icing to pipe a frilled ribbon directly above the first white ribbon. As the petals of this flower are almost continuous and slightly frilled, accentuate the frill by moving the piping nozzle back and forth as you pipe. Once you have piped the blue frill, carefully tap the ends of the iced ribbon with a slightly damp paintbrush to blend them together.

5 Use a slightly damp paintbrush to gently brush the white icing up onto the lower edge of the blue: do not make the paintbrush too damp as this will make the icing too wet. To finish, tap the icing with the side of the paintbrush to blend the two colours together and give the impression of veins.

6 Fit a silicone piping bag with a no. 1.5 nozzle and fill the bag ²/₃ full with soft-peak white royal icing. Pipe five evenly spaced lines from the base of the flower to the top of the blue frill.

7 For the flower centre, colour a small amount of royal icing with Daffodil liquid food colour. Fit a piping bag with a no. 42 nozzle, fill it ²/₃ full with the pale yellow icing and pipe a small cone in the centre of the flower.

8 Gently lift the foil and flower out of the lily nail and set aside to dry on a piece of dimpled foam, or sit the foil in a cupped former. These flowers will take approximately 3–4 days to dry completely depending on the climate.

9 When the flower is completely dry, use a no. 51 leaf nozzle and Leaf Green-coloured royal icing to pipe a calyx onto the back of the flower (see page 109).

tutor tip

Using soft-peak white royal icing and firm-peak blue royal icing means you can achieve a crisp edge to the flower, whilst the icing is still soft enough to blend in.

picture perfect wedding

When it's only an intimate ceremony for your closest friends where a towering wedding cake seems out of place, this small, picture perfect cake is the answer.

iced flowers

15 piped blue morning glories for the main project, see pages 41 to 42, plus a further 2 if you are making the bride and groom's mothers' mini cakes, see page 47

edibles

15cm x 5cm (6" x 2") deep square sponge cake

500g (1lb 1¾oz) buttercream

300g (10½oz) SK Instant Mix Royal Icing

SK Professional Paste Food Colours: Bluebell (Navy Blue), Daffodil (Yellow)

SK Professional Liquid Food Colour: Leaf Green

800g (1lb 12oz) SK Sugarpaste: Bridal White

150g (5¼oz) SK Sugar Dough: Charcoal, White

400g (14oz) SK Mexican Modelling Paste (MMP): White

SK Edible Glue

White vegetable fat or cornflour

Icing sugar in a shaker

equipment

28cm x 35.5cm (11" x 14") rectangular cake drum

SK Great Impressions Rococo Curl Mould

SK Great Impressions Flourish Mould

Small, sharp knife

Piping bag

Piping nozzle: no. 51 (PME)

Palette knife

Greaseproof paper

Scissors

Ruler

Pencil

Paintbrush (SK)

Double-sided tape

Satin ribbon (50mm width): white

1 Using your favourite recipe, bake a 15cm x 5cm deep (6" x 2" deep) square cake, then cut the cake into three tiers in the following sizes:

Top tier: 5cm x 5cm x 5cm (2" x 2" x 2")

Middle tier: 10cm x 5cm x 5cm (4" x 2" x 2")

Bottom tier: 15cm x 5cm x 5cm (6" x 2" x 2")

Once you have cut the tiers from the cake, you will have enough leftover to make another three 5cm x 5cm x 5cm (2" x 2" x 2") cubes. Cut one cube in half and use as edible separators for the tiers.

2 Colour 200g (7oz) of sugarpaste with Bluebell paste colour for the cake drum and 600g (1lb 5¼oz) with Daffodil paste colour for the cake itself. Cover each tier, the edible cake separators and the cake drum in the appropriate colour sugarpaste (see pages 20 to 21).

3 Once you have covered the drum, use a small knife to remove a 2.5cm (1") strip of sugarpaste from each side of the rectangle. Roll out some White MMP to the same depth, cut out four strips to fit around the edges of the rectangle and stick in place with edible glue: these strips will make the picture frame.

4 Do not mount the cakes on the cake drum immediately: arrange each tier, including the edible separators, on a piece of greaseproof paper then carefully draw around the whole cake, making sure you do not touch the cake with the pencil. Move the cake onto a spare board then cut out the outline as a template and position it where you wish the cake to sit on the drum. Use a sharp knife to carefully cut around the template, then remove the spare sugarpaste from the cake drum. Dab a few bulbs of buttercream onto the uncovered part of the cake drum, then assemble the whole cake and stick each tier and the separators in place. The layer of sugarpaste on the drum will help prevent the cake from sliding should you wish to display it standing almost upright.

5 Dust a work surface with icing sugar, roll out some Charcoal Sugar Dough to approximately 3mm (1/8") deep and cut out a piece of paste measuring 18cm x 7cm (7" x 2¾") to represent the wedding cake drum. Attach this to the base of the bottom tier with a little edible glue.

6 On a work surface dusted with icing sugar, roll a long, thin sausage of White Sugar Dough and use edible glue to attach it around the inside edge of the picture frame. Roll another thin sausage and glue it around the bottom tier of the cake so it looks like a small ribbon.

7 Grease your hands with a little white vegetable fat, or dust the Rococo Curl and Flourish moulds with a little cornflour, then use White Sugar Dough in the moulds to make the decoration for the corners of the frame. Use edible glue to attach a Flourish scroll and two Rococo curls to each corner of the frame.

8 Colour some soft-peak royal icing with a little Leaf Green liquid colour, or if desired, colour the icing two different shades of green to create two-tone icing (see page 108). Fit a silicone piping bag with a no. 51 leaf nozzle and fill the bag 2/3 full with green royal icing. Use the green icing to attach six morning glory blooms around the first tier, five around the middle tier and four to the top of the cake. Use the same green icing to pipe leaves between each of the blooms (see page 109).

9 To finish, use double-sided tape to attach the ribbon around the edge of the cake drum. Once the cake is finished, leave it flat for a few hours to ensure that the flowers do not slide out of place.

tutor tips

Decorate the two leftover 5cm (2") cubes of cake to match the main wedding cake and give them as gifts to the mothers of the bride and groom.

You could use an ornate recipe book stand to display the cake at a gentle angle.

tutor tip

For the best results use firm-peak royal icing as this will make the petals stand upwards and outwards from the previous row.

chrysanthemums

edibles

SK Instant Mix Royal Icing

SK Professional Liquid Food Colour:
Leaf Green

equipment

Paper piping bags

Piping nozzles: nos. 51 (PME),
81 (Wilton)

Small palette knife

Wax paper

Flower nail

Paintbrush (SK)

Scissors

1 Fill a small paper piping bag ²/₃ full with firm-peak white royal icing, then cut the tip off the bag. Use a small bulb of royal icing to attach a disc of wax paper to the flower nail, then pipe a rounded bulb of icing that is approximately 5mm (¼") tall in the centre of the paper. If the bulb of royal icing has a peak, use a slightly damp paintbrush to smooth it down whilst the icing is still wet.

2 Fit a piping bag with a no. 81 nozzle and fill the piping bag ²/₃ full with firm-peak white royal icing. With the nozzle end curving upwards, as if smiling, pipe a circle of petals around the base of the central bulb. As you finish piping each petal, gently angle the piping nozzle upward so that the petal curves up at the end.

3 Once you have completed the first circle of petals, pipe slightly shorter petals above the first layer, overlapping the spaces between the previous petals. Continue layering the petals until you reach the centre of the flower, usually seven rows on average. Take care not to dislodge any outer petals as you come closer to the centre of the flower: it can be difficult to fit the last two petals into the small space at the centre. Remove the wax paper with the chrysanthemum from the flower nail and set aside on a flat surface to dry overnight.

4 When dry, peel the chrysanthemum gently off the wax paper, being careful not to break any of the fragile petal tips. To finish, pipe a small calyx onto the back of the chrysanthemum with Leaf Green-coloured royal icing and a no. 51 nozzle (see page 109).

For baby showers, birthdays or anniversaries,
these sweet little parcels make pretty favours
for guests at a special celebration.

beautiful boxes

iced flowers

Chrysanthemums (one flower per box), see
pages 48 to 49

edibles

15cm x 7.5cm x 7.5cm (6" x 3" x 3")
rectangular cake

150g (5¼oz) buttercream for a sponge cake, or
apricot glaze and 250g (8¾oz) marzipan for a
rich fruit cake

SK Instant Mix Royal Icing, approximately 20g
(¾oz) per flower

SK Sugarpaste: 75g (2½oz) Bridal White for
the edible ribbon plus approximately 300g
(10½oz) to cover each cake in the colours of
your choice

SK Professional Paste Food Colours: Bluebell
(Navy Blue), Daffodil (Yellow), Lilac, Nasturtium
(Peach), Rose

Icing sugar in a shaker

SK Edible Glue

equipment

16.5cm x 9cm (6½" x 3½") rectangular thin
cake boards

Small sharp knife or pizza cutting wheel

Small palette knife

Small paintbrush

Piping bag

1 Bake a 15cm (6") square cake from your
favourite recipe, then cut the cake in half to
create two rectangular pieces. Place each cake
onto a cake board and prepare them for covering
with sugarpaste (see pages 17 to 21).

2 Colour 300g (10½oz) of white sugarpaste
with the paste colours of your choice or
use ready-coloured sugarpaste. To achieve the
colours pictured, colour white sugarpaste with a
small amount of Daffodil, Bluebell, Rose, Lilac or
Nasturtium paste colours. Cover each of the cakes
with sugarpaste (see pages 20 to 21).

3 Dust the work surface with more icing
sugar if necessary and roll out some white
sugarpaste to approximately 2mm (⅛") deep. Use
a small sharp knife or pizza wheel to cut out long,
even strips from the paste to make sugarpaste
ribbons. Brush the back of the ribbons with edible
glue and attach along the length and across the
width of each cake.

4 Cut two shorter ribbons that are the same
width as before and use a small sharp knife
to cut a 'V' into one end of each ribbon. Attach the
short ribbons in the centre of the crossed ribbons
to represent the ribbon tails.

5 To finish, fill a piping bag ⅔ full with
soft-peak white royal icing, pipe a small
bulb where the ribbons cross over and attach a
chrysanthemum.

tutor tip

If you don't have time to bake the cakes, you can use a shop-bought Battenberg cake instead as it is the ideal shape for these edible parcels. If you prefer, you can also cut the Battenberg in half widthways to make two square parcels.

water lilies

edibles

SK Instant Mix Royal Icing

SK Professional Liquid Food Colour:
Marigold

SK Professional Dust Food Colour:
Marigold

equipment

Food-grade card or thin plastic for stencils

Craft knife

Curved former e.g. flower former, apple tray
or cardboard tube cut in half lengthways

Wax paper

Small palette knife

Scissors

Silicone piping bags

Piping nozzles: nos. 1.5, 4 (PME)

Fine paintbrush (SK)

Dusting brush (SK)

Templates, see page 110

1 Make your own stencils for each different-sized petal by drawing around the templates on page 110. Once you have drawn four petal shapes on separate pieces of card or thin plastic, cut them out carefully with a craft knife. You only need three different-sized petals to make a basic lily, but having a fourth petal size gives you the option to make lilies in varying sizes.

2 Cut pieces of wax paper that are large enough for the individual petals and place under the stencils. Make up some soft-peak white royal icing and spread the icing through the stencil using a piece of food-grade card or plastic as a spreader. Gently lift the stencil away from the wax paper to give the petals a clean edge.

3 While the icing is still wet, place the petals in a curved former such as a flower former or a cardboard tube cut in half lengthways to give the petals a gentle curve. Repeat to make as many petals as required in different sizes; the number of petals is a personal choice but I prefer to use 8 large petals, 8 medium petals and 8 small

petals plus a few spares in each size to allow for breakages. Leave the petals for approximately two hours until they are completely dry.

4 Once dry, peel the wax paper away from the petals and group them according to size. Use a dusting brush to dust inside the base of each petal with Marigold dust colour. Colour some soft-peak royal icing with Marigold liquid food colour: try to match the colour of the icing to the colour of the dusted petals. Fit a silicone piping bag with a no. 1.5 piping nozzle and fill the bag $^2/_3$ full with the Marigold-coloured icing.

5 Cut a circle of wax paper that is approximately 2.5cm (1") in diameter and place it in the base of a cupped former e.g. an apple tray. Use bulbs of yellow royal icing to attach an outer circle of the largest petals to the wax paper. Once the petals are firmly attached, use a dry paintbrush to tidy up any royal icing between the petals.

6 Create an inner circle with the medium petals: attach them to the larger petals with bulbs of the coloured royal icing so that they sit between the gaps in the first row of petals. Repeat for the smaller petals, then fill in the central area where the petals meet with soft-peak royal icing to secure all the petals in place. You can change the size of the final lily by varying the number of rows of petals.

7 When the lily is completely dry, fit a silicone piping bag with a no. 4 nozzle then fill the bag $^2/_3$ full with Marigold-coloured, firm-peak royal icing. Pipe a cone in the centre of the water lily and smooth down the peak with a damp paintbrush if necessary.

8 Colour some more firm-peak royal icing with Marigold liquid colour so that it is a darker shade than the cone in the centre. Fit a silicone piping bag with a no. 1.5 nozzle then fill the bag $^2/_3$ full with the yellow royal icing. Starting at the base, pipe very small spikes over the cone until the whole cone is covered. Leave the water lily to dry for 24 hours before removing it from the wax paper.

tutor tips

It is a good idea to leave the lily to dry for at least 30 minutes between each layer of petals, so that the previous row of petals does not move while you are attaching the next row.

Water lilies can either be assembled directly onto a cake or made on a piece of wax paper and attached later. If you create the flower on wax paper first, use a cupped former such as an apple tray to help the petals maintain their curve.

water lily pond

This art-inspired cake would be perfect for a silver, gold, emerald or ruby wedding anniversary, just change the colour of the dragonflies to match the celebration.

iced flowers

3 water lilies, see pages 55 to 57
Dragonfly, see pages 63 to 64

edibles

10cm and 20.5cm (4" and 8") square cakes

800g (1lb 12oz) buttercream for sponge cakes, or apricot glaze and 1.14kg (2½lb) marzipan for rich fruit cakes

1.35kg (3lb) SK Sugarpaste: Bridal White

250g (8¾oz) SK Instant Mix Royal Icing

SK Professional Paste Food Colour: Bluegrass

SK Professional Liquid Food Colours: Bluegrass or Vine

SK Designer Metallic Lustre Dust Food Colour: Classic Gold

SK Professional Dust Food Colours: Bluegrass, Fern

SK Sugar Dough: Charcoal

SK Confectioners' Glaze

250g (8¾oz) bag SK Instant Mix Pastillage Powder

Icing sugar in a shaker

Cornflour

equipment

10cm and 20.5cm (4" and 8") square thin cake boards

30.5cm (12") square cake drum

4 cake dowels

Small, clean food-grade sponge or kitchen paper

Small, flat paintbrush (SK)

Paint palette or small dish

Craft knife

Satin ribbon: dark blue/green to complement the bluegrass colour of the cake

Double-sided tape

SK Glaze Cleaner (IPA)

1 Bake the cakes using your favourite recipe, prepare them for covering (see pages 17 to 21) and place them on the corresponding thin cake boards. Colour all of the sugarpaste turquoise with Bluegrass paste food colour and cover the cakes and drum.

2 In a paint palette or small dish, mix a little Classic Gold lustre dust with confectioners' glaze until you achieve a smooth consistency. Use a small, flat paintbrush and the gold mixture to paint random crescent shapes around the base of each tier, representing fish in the pond.

3 Mix a little Bluegrass dust with confectioners' glaze, then dip a small piece of clean, food-grade sponge or a piece of crumpled kitchen paper into the mixture. Mark on the cake drum where the base tier will be positioned then blot the sponge

or paper around the bottom of each tier and around the inside edge of the cake drum (where the base tier will be) to create a dappled effect.

4 Following the instructions on the packet, make up some pastillage from the mix. On a work surface dusted with cornflour, roll out 24 long, thin sausages of pastillage to make the reeds. Taper and curl the ends to give movement, then lay the reeds on a piece of kitchen paper or foam and leave to dry overnight. Once dry, dust Bluegrass over the bottom half of the reeds and Fern towards the top.

5 Position the base tier on the cake drum so it sits at a 45° angle to the cake drum and use a few bulbs of royal icing to secure it in place. To support the top tier insert four dowels into the bottom tier: push each dowel down to the base of the cake, ensuring they are within the size and position of the upper tier, then mark each dowel where it is level with the sugarpaste. Remove all the dowels, cut them at the mark with a craft knife, then re-insert them into the cake. Place the top tier towards the back corner of the base tier and use a few bulbs of royal icing to secure it.

6 Place the dark green ribbon around the cake drum and use double-sided tape to stick the ends of the ribbon together where they overlap at the back of the cake to secure it in place.

7 Cluster five or six reeds together, then use some firm-peak royal icing to stick the reeds to the cake drum or insert them directly into the sugarpaste on the top and bottom tiers. To support the reeds and keep them in position, mould small pebbles from Charcoal Sugar Dough that has been mixed with a little Fern dust food colour and stick them in place with a dab of royal icing.

8 Carefully attach one water lily to each tier and one to the drum with small bulbs of royal icing. Once the reeds are secure, colour some firm-peak royal icing with Bluegrass or Vine liquid colours to match the reeds and use this to attach a dragonfly to a reed on the top tier. You may have to hold the dragonfly in place for a few moments whilst the royal icing hardens.

tutor tips

If you are transporting the cake, it is wise to attach any delicate pieces, such as dragonflies, at the venue as this will reduce the chance of breakages.

To achieve the best results, colour the sugarpaste in natural light 24 hours ahead of use as the colour may change slightly as it develops.

dragonflies

edibles

SK Instant Mix Royal Icing

SK Professional Liquid Food Colour of your choice

SK Designer Metallic Lustre Dust Food Colour of your choice

SK Designer Fairy Sparkles Dust: Ice White

SK Confectioners' Glaze

equipment

Card or thin food-grade plastic for stencils

Craft knife

Wax paper

Piping bag

Piping nozzle: no. 3 (PME)

Small palette knife

Scissors

Fine paintbrush (SK)

SK Glaze Cleaner (IPA)

Templates, see page 110

1 Make your own stencils for the dragonfly wings by drawing around the templates on page 110. Once you have drawn the dragonfly wings on a piece of card or thin plastic, cut them out carefully with a craft knife. You will only need one of each wing stencil as you can turn it over to create identical opposite wings. Cut pieces of wax paper large enough for the wings and place under the stencils. Make up some white soft-peak royal icing, then spread the icing through the stencil using a piece of food-grade card or plastic as a spreader.

2 Gently lift the stencil away from the wax paper to give the wings a clean edge, then immediately sprinkle them with Ice White Fairy Sparkles to add shimmer to the wings. Tap off any excess sparkles and then leave the wings

on a flat surface to dry. Repeat to make as many pairs of dragonfly wings as required, making sure that you have equal numbers of both left and right wings. Leave the wings to dry completely for approximately two hours. Once the wings are dry, peel away the wax paper and sort them into matching pairs.

3 Cut a piece of wax paper approximately the size of a business card. Fold lengthways 5mm (^{1}/$_8$") in from the two long edges to create shallow 'walls': the wing tips will rest on these when attached to the body to lift them slightly.

4 Make up some firm-peak royal icing and colour it with the liquid food colour of your choice for the body. Fit a silicone piping bag with a no. 3 piping nozzle and fill the bag ^{2}/$_3$ full with firm-peak royal icing. Pipe a long rope down the centre of the wax paper for the dragonfly's tail: start at the end of the tail and finish where the tail would join the body. Pipe a long teardrop for the body, making sure that it is touching the tail.

5 Gently rest the smaller back wings on the body, then apply a little pressure with a dry paintbrush to insert them into the body, using the wax paper 'walls' to support them. Repeat for the longer front wings. Use the no. 3 nozzle and firm-peak royal icing to pipe a bulb for the head and

two smaller bulbs for the eyes. Set the whole piece aside to dry for 24 hours.

6 When the dragonfly is dry, gently peel away the wax paper. To paint the body, mix a small amount of confectioners' glaze with the metallic lustre dust colours of your choice and paint with a fine paintbrush. As you have piped the body with coloured royal icing, the dust colour mixture will allow you to get better coverage than painting onto white icing.

Note: As soon as you have finished painting the dragonfly, wash the brush in glaze cleaner, then rinse it with clean, warm water to prevent any damage to the bristles.

tutor tip

To achieve a realistic look, the dragonfly tail should be no shorter than the longest wing when measured from the end of the body to the tip of the tail.

christmas roses

edibles

SK Instant Mix Royal Icing

SK Professional Liquid Food Colour:
Daffodil (Yellow)

SK Professional Dust Food Colour: Vine

SK Pollen Style Edible Dust Food Colour:
Pale Yellow

equipment

Piping bags

Piping nozzles: nos. 2, 56 (PME)

Small palette knife

Flower nail

Wax paper

Round paintbrush (SK)

Small dusting brush (SK)

Air puffer (optional)

1 Make up some white firm-peak royal icing, fit a silicone piping bag with a no. 56 petal nozzle, then fill the bag ²/₃ full with the icing. Attach a piece of wax paper to the head of a flower nail with a small touch of royal icing.

2 Holding the flower nail between your thumb and index finger, roll the nail in an anticlockwise direction (or clockwise direction if you are left handed). At the same time pipe a very small arch with the petal nozzle. Make sure that you start and finish the petal in the centre of the nail and keep the arch narrow: there should be no gap in the centre of the petal.

3 Continue to pipe four more petals in a circle from the same central point. It is important to stop in between each petal as this will give the final flower more definition. When you pipe the fifth and final petal, lift the piping nozzle directly upward to finish it and then reposition the edge of the last petal against the first with a dry paintbrush. Whilst the Christmas rose is still wet, tidy up its centre with a dry paintbrush. Lift the

christmas roses

disc of wax paper off the flower nail and leave the flower to dry.

4 When the Christmas rose is completely dry, use a small, dry dusting brush to dust the area around its centre with Vine dust colour. Use a puffer to remove any excess dust from the flower.

5 To finish the Christmas rose, colour a small amount of soft-peak royal icing with Daffodil liquid food colour. Fit a silicone piping bag with a no. 2 nozzle and fill it $^2/_3$ full with the yellow icing. Pipe a small bulb in the centre of the flower where the petals meet. Immediately sprinkle Pale Yellow edible pollen over the centre of the Christmas rose, tap off the excess pollen and leave to dry completely before removing it from the wax paper.

tutor tip

If you do not have an air puffer for removing excess dust you can use a small plastic bottle with a small aperture, such as a small squeezy bottle. Make sure that the bottle is completely clean and dry before you use it.

poinsettias

edibles

SK Instant Mix Royal Icing

SK Professional Liquid Food Colour:
Sunflower

SK Professional Dust Food Colour:
Poinsettia (Christmas Red)

equipment

Silicone piping bags

Piping nozzles: nos. 1, 2 (PME)

Wax paper

Small palette knife

Small round paintbrush (SK)

Dimpled foam or kitchen paper

1 Make up some soft-peak royal icing and colour with Poinsettia dust food colour; dust food colours are recommended when you want to make the royal icing an intense, deep colour. Fit a silicone piping bag with a no. 2 nozzle then fill the bag ²/₃ full with the red icing. Cut a small piece of wax paper large enough for a poinsettia bract: if the sides of the wax paper curl up from being on a roll don't worry as you can use this to help give the flower a natural curve.

2 Pressure pipe a line that is tapered at each end onto the wax paper as shown in the step photograph: make it narrow at one end, then increase the pressure in the middle and taper off again towards the tip. Immediately pipe another identical tapered line next to the first as shown, so

that the sides are completely touching. The join down the centre will make the bract's central vein.

3 Whilst the royal icing is still wet, use a fine paintbrush to stroke the icing into points around the edge of each bract. Leave the bract on the wax paper, allowing the sides of the paper to curl up, and set aside to dry on a piece of dimpled foam or crumpled kitchen paper for a couple of hours. Make several bracts in different sizes to make the poinsettia look natural: I usually use between 6 and 10 bracts to make a full poinsettia depending on the size of the flower.

4 Once completely dry, gently remove the bracts from the wax paper, being careful not to damage the pointed ends. To attach the

poinsettia to a cake, pipe a small circle of red royal icing where you want the poinsettia to sit. Push the ends of the bracts into it to form a circle.

5 To finish the flower, colour some soft-peak royal icing with a touch of Sunflower liquid colour. Fit a silicone piping bag with a no. 1 nozzle then fill the bag 2/3 full with the yellow icing. Pipe a cluster of small dots in the middle of the bracts to create the flower centre and push a second layer of bracts into the wet icing to secure them in place.

festive chocolate rolls

Pre-piped iced flowers are a quick and easy way to make any dessert look impressive. Perfect if you're short on time this Christmas, just dress up some shop-bought chocolate rolls with festive iced flowers for quick treats that will look great on your party table.

iced flowers

Christmas roses, see pages 65 to 67

Poinsettias, see pages 68 to 70

Holly leaves, see page 70

edibles

Chocolate-coated mini Swiss rolls

SK Instant Mix Royal Icing, approximately 10g (¼oz) per mini roll

SK Fairy Sparkles Dust Food Colour: Ice White or icing sugar (optional)

equipment

Piping bag

Small paintbrush

Tea strainer (optional)

tutor tip

Once you have decorated the mini Swiss rolls with royal icing, do not put them in the refrigerator.

1 Either make or purchase some chocolate-coated mini Swiss rolls. Be careful not to leave fingerprints on them as you handle them.

2 Make up some royal icing to run-out consistency, fill a paper piping bag ⅔ full and cut off the tip of the bag (no nozzle required). Pipe a small area of white icing at one end of the mini Swiss roll and use a small paintbrush to encourage the wet icing to run down the sides of the chocolate roll if necessary. Leave to dry for an hour.

3 Carefully arrange your chosen iced flowers on the royal iced area and attach them with small bulbs of white royal icing. Use a small paintbrush to manipulate the flowers and leaves into position and leave to dry.

4 Just before you serve, use a tea strainer (or similar) to sprinkle a small amount of icing sugar or SK Fairy Sparkles dust over each of the rolls for a snowy effect.

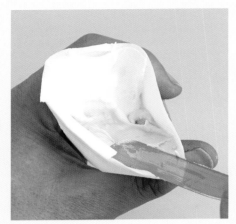

petunias

edibles

SK Instant Mix Royal Icing

SK Professional Liquid Food Colours:
Leaf Green and two other colours of
your choice

White vegetable fat

equipment

Piping bags

Piping nozzles: no. 2 (PME);
no. 104 (Wilton)

Small palette knife

Kitchen foil

Lily nail: 4cm (1½") (Wilton)

Round paintbrush (SK)

Scissors

Dimpled foam or crumpled
kitchen paper

1 Make up some firm-peak royal icing, divide into two bowls and colour with two different but complementary liquid food colours of your choice. Fit a piping bag with a no. 104 petal nozzle. Pick up a small amount of the darker coloured royal icing on a small palette knife and place down one side of the piping bag. Repeat with the lighter-coloured royal icing and place down the other side of the bag. When you pipe, the royal icing will be two-toned.

2 Cut out a square of kitchen foil and smear the shiny side with white vegetable fat. Push the foil into the lily nail with the shiny side facing upwards. Wrap the edge of the foil over the lip of the nail to help hold it in place whilst piping.

3 Using the widest part of the nozzle to make the base of the petal, start piping a petal from down in the middle of the lily nail, then move upwards to the lip and back down again. The petals of a petunia are quite wide and frilled, so move the piping nozzle back and forth as you pipe and try to curve the top of the petal over the lip of the nail.

4 Continue to pipe all five petals individually, ensuring you stop piping after each petal.

If you pipe all the petals in one motion it will allow the icing to build up at the base of the flower, lengthening the drying time and reducing the depth of the trumpet.

5 Use a slightly damp paintbrush to smooth over the joins at the base of the petals and remove any excess royal icing. Gently lift the foil out of the lily nail and set it aside on a piece of dimpled foam or sit it on crumpled kitchen paper. Repeat to make as many flowers as required then leave to dry for approximately 3–5 days depending on the climate (higher humidity will increase drying time).

6 Once the petunias are completely dry, gently peel the foil away from the flower. Colour a small amount of firm-peak royal icing with Leaf Green liquid food colour. Fit a piping bag with a no. 2 nozzle, fill the bag ²/₃ full with the green royal icing and pipe five smaller cones around one larger cone to represent the stamens of the flower.

7 To attach the flower to a cake or cupcake, pipe a calyx onto the back of the petunia (see instructions on page 109) and position the flower whilst the icing is still wet.

tutor tips

If you find the petals are not lying flat, use an air puffer to gently blow them down before you remove the foil from the lily nail.

To add variety to the petunias using the same colour combinations, just twist the nozzle around in the end of the piping bag. The new position of the nozzle will adjust how the colours of the icing blend together.

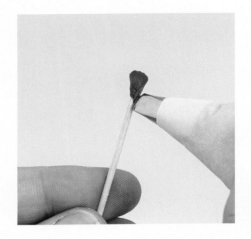

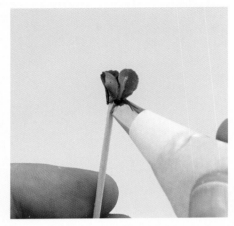

cornflowers

edibles

SK Instant Mix Royal Icing

SK Professional Liquid Food Colours:
Bluebell (Navy Blue), Hyacinth,
Leaf Green

equipment

Cocktail stick

Piping bag

Piping nozzles: nos. 50, 57S (PME)

Small palette knife

Wax paper squares

1 Colour some firm-peak royal icing with Bluebell and Hyacinth liquid food colours to achieve the vibrant blue of a traditional cornflower. Fit a piping bag with a no. 57S nozzle and fill it ⅔ full with the blue royal icing. Hold a cocktail stick between your index finger and thumb and, with the widest part of the nozzle at the base, pipe a blade-like petal at the tip of the cocktail stick: this is achieved by attaching the royal icing to the cocktail stick then piping in an upwards and downwards motion, staying in contact with the cocktail stick all the time.

2 Pipe blade-like petals on either side of the first petal. As you finish each petal, wipe the nozzle down the cocktail stick to keep the nozzle clean and the petals neat. Continue to pipe individual petals outside the first three petals: tilt

your hand to make it easier to finish each petal where it meets the cocktail stick.

3 Pipe enough petals to make the cornflower the desired size, then push a square of wax paper up the cocktail stick to sit underneath the flower. Supporting the flower with your fingers, remove the cocktail stick with a gentle twisting motion to tighten the centre of the flower: this will prevent a hole appearing in the middle of the flower. Leave the flowers to dry for approximately 24 hours.

4 Once completely dry, remove the cornflower from the wax paper. To attach the flower to a cake or cupcake, pipe a calyx onto the back of the cornflower with Leaf Green-coloured royal icing (see instructions on page 109) and position the flower whilst the icing is still wet.

garden gems wedding cake

This pretty wedding cake is perfect for a summer ceremony as it is vibrant, colourful and the butterflies add a fun twist.

iced flowers

16 cornflowers, see pages 76 to 77

24 petunias: Daffodil and Marigold, Nasturtium and Thrift, White and Rose, White and Hyacinth, see pages 72 to 75

7 butterflies: Daffodil, Fuchsia, Marigold, Thrift, Wisteria, see pages 82 to 83

edibles

10cm (4") round cake and 15cm and 25.5cm (6" and 10") square cakes, prepared for covering, see pages 17 to 21

500g (1lb 1¾oz) bag SK Instant Mix Royal Icing

2.5kg (5lb 8¼oz) SK Sugarpaste: Bridal White

SK Professional Paste Food Colour: Nasturtium (Peach)

SK Professional Liquid Food Colour: Leaf Green

equipment

10cm (4") round thin cake board

15cm and 25.5cm (6" and 10") square thin cake boards

35.5cm (14") square cake drum

8 cake dowels

Piping bag

Piping nozzle: no. 52

Small palette knife

Craft knife

Double-sided tape

Satin ribbons: champagne (50mm width); green, orange (15mm width)

1 Bake the cakes from your favourite recipe, prepare them for covering and place them on the corresponding thin cake board. Colour the sugarpaste with Nasturtium paste food colour, then cover the cakes and cake drum with the peach-coloured sugarpaste (see pages 17 to 21).

2 Secure the bottom tier to the cake drum with a few bulbs of royal icing. Insert four dowels into the cake within the size and shape of the middle tier and mark them level with the sugarpaste. Remove the dowels, cut them to length with a craft knife and then re-insert them into the cake. Place the middle tier so that it sits at a 45° angle to the base tier, securing it in place with bulbs of royal icing. Dowel the middle tier and attach the top tier in the same way.

3 Trim the cake drum with bright green ribbon and

secure in place at the back of the drum with double-sided tape. Attach champagne ribbon around the bottom of the base and top tiers with royal icing, then overlay this with the orange ribbon.

4 Colour some soft-peak royal icing with Leaf Green liquid food colour. Fit a piping bag with a no. 52 leaf nozzle then fill the bag $^2/_3$ full with soft-peak green royal icing, making it two-toned if desired (see page 108). Pipe leaves around the top corners of the base tier (see page 109) and use these to stick the cornflowers and petunias in place. Attach approximately six petunias to each corner of the first tier and arrange in a triangle.

5 Once the flowers are firmly attached to the cake, stick the butterflies in place with firm-peak royal icing. You may have to hold the butterflies in place for a few seconds as the royal icing hardens. If the cake is to be transported, it is a good idea to attach the butterflies at the venue.

tutor tip

If you find that the flowers don't have enough height once arranged on the cake, attach a large teardrop of sugarpaste to the cake and secure the flowers to the paste. You could also pipe a large rope of royal icing and stick the flowers to this; neither the paste nor the rope of icing will be seen once the flowers are in position.

garden gems cupcakes

edibles

600g (1lb 5¼oz) vanilla buttercream

12 cupcakes made using a recipe of your choice

12 two-tone petunias, see pages 72 to 75

equipment

SK Polka Dot Cupcake Cases: Sorbet Collection

Large plastic piping bag

Savoy piping nozzle: no. 9 star

1 Bake a batch of cupcakes using your favourite recipe.

2 Once the cupcakes are completely cooled pipe a generous swirl of vanilla buttercream on top of each using a plastic no. 9 Savoy star piping nozzle and a large plastic piping bag.

3 Place a single two-toned petunia on top of the buttercream swirl before serving.

tutor tip

Attaching the flowers only an hour before serving will ensure that the royal icing stays firm and that the moisture from the buttercream does not get absorbed into the flower.

butterflies

edibles

SK Instant Mix Royal Icing

SK Professional Liquid Food Colour of your choice

White vegetable fat

equipment

Card or thin food-grade plastic for stencils

Craft knife

Piping bags

Piping nozzles: nos. 2, 3 (PME)

Small palette knife

Wax paper or cellophane

Scissors

Fine paintbrush (SK)

Seed head stamens, glitter tipped, small (optional)

Templates, see page 110

1   Make your own stencils for the butterfly wings by drawing around the templates on page 110. Once you have drawn the wing on a piece of card or thin plastic, cut it out carefully with a craft knife. You will only need one wing stencil as you can turn it over to create the identical opposite wing.

2   Cut several pieces of wax paper or cellophane large enough for the wings, lightly smear them with white vegetable fat and place under the stencil. Make up some soft-peak royal icing and colour it with the liquid food colour of your choice. Spread the icing through the stencil with a piece of card or plastic as a spreader. Gently lift the stencil away from the wax paper to give the wing a clean edge. Place the wing on a flat surface and leave to dry. Repeat to make as many butterfly wings as required, making sure you have equal numbers of both left and right wings. Leave the wings to dry overnight if possible.

3 Once completely dry, peel the wax paper or cellophane from the wings and line them up in matching pairs. Colour some royal icing with the liquid food colour of your choice, fit a piping bag with a no. 2 piping nozzle and fill the bag 2/3 full. Pipe the wing design of your choice, then tidy up the ends of the piped lines with a slightly damp paintbrush if necessary.

4 Cut a piece of card approximately the size of a playing card and fold it in half lengthwise: this will be the former on which to dry the butterfly. Re-use a piece of wax paper or cellophane, fold it in half, then lay it in the folded piece of card.

5 Make up some firm-peak royal icing and colour it with the liquid food colour of your choice for the body. Fit a silicone piping bag with a no. 3 nozzle and fill the bag to 2/3 full with the coloured icing. Pipe a long teardrop into the crease in the wax paper to create the butterfly's body. Gently insert the wings into either side of the body using the card to support them.

6 Whilst the icing is still wet, insert two flower stamens into the head to look like antennae, then leave the butterflies to dry for several hours. Once dry, remove them from the wax paper and attach them to the cake with a small bulb of royal icing.

Note: If the butterflies are going to be eaten, omit the stamens as they are not edible. If they are not going to be eaten, make sure the butterflies are removed before the cake is served.

tutor tip

To create a dotty design on the butterfly wings, lightly smear a piece of cellophane with white vegetable fat and pipe small run-out dots onto it. Once they are dry, you can paint them with a combination of confectioners' glaze and metallic lustre dust before attaching them to the wings with a touch of royal icing to give your creations added drama.

forget-me-nots

edibles

SK Instant Mix Royal Icing

SK Professional Liquid Food Colours:
Bluebell (Navy Blue), Daffodil (Yellow),
Gentian (Ice Blue)

equipment

Card or thin, food-grade plastic for
stencils

Craft knife

Wax paper

Scissors

Piping bags

Piping nozzle: no. 2 (PME)

Small palette knife

Fine paintbrush (SK)

Small pieces of foam or kitchen paper

Pointed tweezers (optional)

Template see page 110

Teardrop paper craft punch (optional)

1 Make your own stencils for the petals by drawing around the templates on page 110. Once you have drawn the petals on a piece of card or thin plastic, cut it out carefully with a craft knife. Cutting several petal shapes into the same piece of card or plastic will speed up how many petals you can make in one go.

2 Colour some soft-peak royal icing to the desired shade of blue with Bluebell and Gentian liquid food colours. Cut pieces of wax paper large enough for a strip of petals, place under the stencil, then spread the blue icing through the stencil with a piece of card or food-

grade plastic as a spreader. Gently lift the stencil away from the wax paper to give the petals clean edges. Place the flower on the wax paper to one side to dry. Repeat to make as many petals as required: one forget-me-not flower has five petals. It is a good idea to make spare petals at this stage in case of breakages. Leave the petals to dry completely for a couple of hours, then carefully peel the wax paper from the petals.

3 Make up some firm-peak blue royal icing the same colour as the petals. Fit a silicone piping bag with a no. 2 piping nozzle and fill the bag 2/3 full with the blue icing. Pipe a small bulb

of icing onto a piece of wax paper, insert five forget-me-not petals into the bulb and use a dry paintbrush to manipulate them into place. These petals may need a little support, so use tiny pieces of foam or kitchen paper to keep them in place. Leave to dry for several hours.

4 Colour some soft-peak royal icing with a touch of Daffodil liquid colour to make pale yellow icing. Fit a piping bag with a no. 2 piping nozzle and fill the bag $^2/_3$ full with the icing. Pipe a small, yellow bulb in the middle of the flower and touch down any peaks with a damp paintbrush if necessary.

5 To attach a forget-me-not to a cake, pipe a small leaf where you wish the flower to sit (see page 109), then pick the flower up by its centre with pointed tweezers and carefully place in position.

tutor tips

If you are a paper crafter, you may already have a teardrop-shaped craft punch which you can use to cut out the petal stencil.

As forget-me-nots are very fragile, it is sometimes easier to make them directly onto the cake. However, if you do prepare them on wax paper beforehand make sure you use a pair of pointed tweezers and pick them up by their centres.

something blue

The little forget-me-nots add a touch of colour to this elegant wedding dress design. Make this sophisticated cake for a bridal shower, hen party or a first anniversary or even as an alternative wedding cake.

iced flowers

15–20 forget-me-nots, see pages 84 to 86

edibles

Sponge cake baked in a 20.5cm (8") Tiffin tin or pudding basin

300g (10½oz) buttercream

100g (3½oz) SK Instant Mix Royal Icing

570g (1lb 4oz) SK Sugarpaste: Bridal White

100g (3½oz) SK Sugar Dough: Soft Beige

SK Professional Paste Food Colour: Leaf Green

SK Professional Liquid Food Colour: Leaf Green

SK Edible Glue

Icing sugar in a shaker

equipment

25.5cm (10") oval cake drum

20.5cm (8") Tiffin tin (optional)

Small, sharp knife

Small paintbrush for edible glue

Kitchen paper

Dowel

Rolling pin

Piping bag

Piping nozzle: no. 51 (PME)

Small palette knife

Fluted edge cutter

Double-sided tape

Satin ribbon (50mm): blue

1 Bake your favourite sponge cake recipe in a Tiffin tin or a pudding basin to achieve the basic shape for the dress. Trim down the sides of the cake with a serrated knife to create a narrower body shape, then layer and crumb-coat the cake and place in a refrigerator to firm for fifteen minutes.

2 Colour some white sugarpaste with a touch of Leaf Green paste colour and cover the cake drum.

3 Roll out some white sugarpaste to approximately 3mm (1/8") deep and wrap the sugarpaste around the cake, making sure that the sugarpaste is in full contact with the buttercream coating. Place the cake onto the cake drum and smooth down the sugarpaste with cake smoothers or the palm of your hand.

4 For the skirt, roll out a large oval of white sugarpaste to approximately 1–2mm (just under $^1/_8$") thick, measuring around 38cm (15") long. Place over the coated cake and secure at the waistline with a little edible glue. Use pieces of kitchen paper to support the waves in the hem of the dress until they have completely dried: the waves in the hem need to be large enough to go over one or two forget-me-not flowers.

5 Take 75g (2½oz) of Soft Beige Sugar Dough, mould it into a rectangular shape that is approximately 7cm (2¾") long and in proportion to the skirt, then pinch it in at the middle to create the waist. Attach the torso to the skirt with a touch of edible glue and whilst it is still soft, insert a dowel down through the torso, into the cake and all the way to the drum. Mark the dowel, remove from the cake and cut off any excess with a craft knife, then re-insert into the torso. This may distort the torso slightly so gently re-shape it if necessary. Mould a small piece of Sugar Dough for the neck of the dressmaker's mannequin and place it over the hole where the dowel was inserted. You can add a small sugar ribbon or string of edible beads around it later to conceal the join.

6 Dust a work surface with icing sugar and roll out some white sugarpaste for the bodice of the dress. Cut a strip of paste approximately 5cm x 10cm (2" x 4"), and whilst the paste is still damp wrap it around the body and carefully trim it to size using a small sharp knife. Once you are happy with the fit attach it using edible glue. Cut a further strip

of paste approximately 5mm ($^1/_8$") wide and attach this over the join at the back of the bodice. Attach small balls of paste for the buttons. To create the top of the bodice cut a strip of paste with a fluted cutter and attach with edible glue.

7 To make a bow for the back of the dress, cut a thin strip of white sugarpaste. Cut two equal lengths for the loops, a shorter piece for the knot and two long ribbon tails with a 'V' shape in the end. Gently fold over the loops then glue each piece in position on the back of the dress, pleating the paste in the centre of the bow to create a fabric effect. Finish the dress by adding your own choice of finer details such as frills and buttons.

8 Attach blue ribbon around the edge of the cake drum with double-sided tape. Colour some royal icing with Leaf Green liquid colour and pipe leaves in the gaps under the hem (see page 109). Use pointed tweezers to attach the forget-me-nots to the leaves whilst they are still wet.

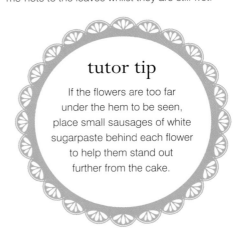

tutor tip

If the flowers are too far under the hem to be seen, place small sausages of white sugarpaste behind each flower to help them stand out further from the cake.

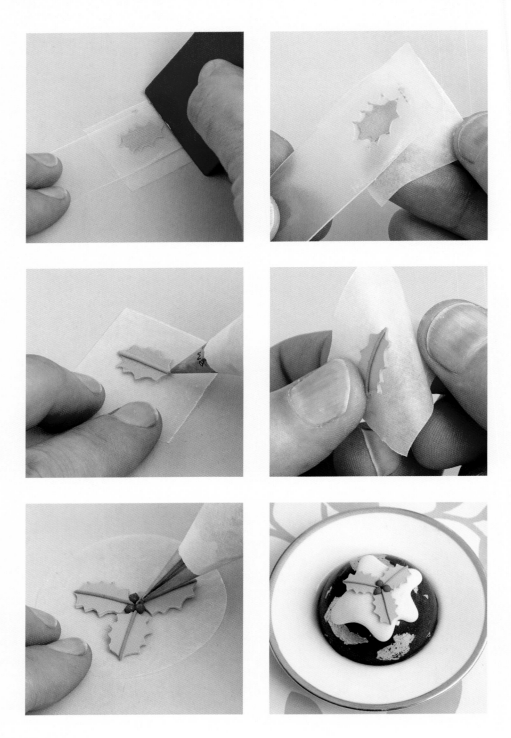

holly and berries

edibles

SK Instant Mix Royal Icing

SK Professional Liquid Food Colours: Holly/Ivy (Dark Green), Leaf Green, Poinsettia (Christmas Red)

equipment

Card or thin, food-grade plastic for stencils

Craft knife

Wax paper

Scissors

Piping bags

Piping nozzle: no. 1 (PME)

Small palette knife

Fine paintbrush (SK)

Dimpled foam or crumpled kitchen paper

Holly leaf paper craft punch (optional)

Template, see page 110

1 Make your own stencils for the leaves by drawing around the template on page 110. Once you have drawn the leaf on a piece of card or thin plastic, cut it out carefully with a craft knife.

2 Cut pieces of wax paper large enough for the leaf shapes. Colour some soft-peak royal icing with Holly/Ivy and Leaf Green liquid food colours then spread the green royal icing over the stencil using a piece of card or food-grade plastic as a spreader. Gently lift the stencil away from the wax paper to give the leaf a clean edge. Leave the leaf on the wax paper and place on a piece of

dimpled foam or crumpled kitchen paper to dry. Repeat to make as many holly leaves as required. Leave the holly leaves for a couple of hours until they are completely dry.

3 Colour some soft-peak royal icing a darker shade of green than the holly leaves. Fit a piping bag with a no. 1 piping nozzle and fill the bag 2/3 full with the green icing. Pipe a line down the centre of the holly leaf and tidy up the ends of the line with a dry paintbrush, if necessary. This central line will strengthen the holly leaf. Once the leaf is completely dry, peel off the wax paper.

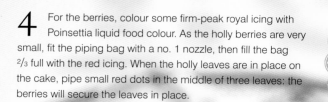

4 For the berries, colour some firm-peak royal icing with Poinsettia liquid food colour. As the holly berries are very small, fit the piping bag with a no. 1 nozzle, then fill the bag $2/3$ full with the red icing. When the holly leaves are in place on the cake, pipe small red dots in the middle of three leaves: the berries will secure the leaves in place.

tutor tip

If you are a paper crafter, you may already have a holly leaf craft punch which you can use to cut out the leaf stencil.

chocolate christmas puddings

If you're not a fan of traditional Christmas pudding, then these individual chocolate desserts are a wonderfully indulgent alternative and can be dressed up with iced holly and berries for a festive touch.

iced flowers

3 holly leaves per pudding, see pages 92 to 94

edibles

No-bake chocolate Christmas puddings, see recipe on page 23

SK Instant Mix Royal Icing, approximately 5g (less than ¼oz) per pudding

SK Edible Gold Leaf

SK Easy Melt Choc Coating: White, approximately 10g (¼oz) per pudding

SK Professional Liquid Food Colour: Poinsettia (Christmas Red)

equipment

Small paintbrush

Silikomart medium (50mm) half-sphere silicone mould

Spoon

1 Make sure that the half-sphere silicone mould is clean and dry, then use a small, dry paintbrush to place pieces of edible gold leaf into the bottom of each half-sphere. Brush down the gold leaf so that it is in full contact with the mould.

2 Prepare the no-bake chocolate Christmas puddings in the half-sphere silicone moulds, following the recipe on page 23.

3 Melt a little Easy Melt Choc Coating following the instructions on the packet. Once melted, use a spoon to drizzle the coating over the top of each pudding, then place them back in the refrigerator to chill.

4 Remove from the refrigerator approximately 30 minutes before serving. Place three holly leaves on top of each pudding and stick them in place with a little royal icing. Colour some firm-peak royal icing with Poinsettia liquid colour and pipe three berries in the middle of the leaves (see opposite), then serve.

magnolia

edibles

SK Instant Mix Royal Icing

SK Professional Liquid Food Colour: Cyclamen

SK Professional Dust Food Colour: Rose

SK Designer Pastel Dust Food Colour:
Soft Yellow

SK Sugar Florist Paste (SFP): Pale Yellow

White vegetable fat

equipment

Piping bags

Piping nozzles: nos. 1 (PME), 104 (Wilton)

Small palette knife

Wax paper

Flower nail (optional)

Curved petal former (optional)

Kitchen paper or pieces of foam

Dusting brushes

Small paintbrush

Small pointed scissors

Cocktail stick

Air puffer

1 Make up some firm-peak royal icing, fit a piping bag with a no. 104 petal nozzle then fill the bag 2/3 full with the white icing. Attach a square of wax paper to the head of a flower nail with a small touch of royal icing: you don't have to use a flower nail but it does makes it easier to manipulate the nozzle when piping the petals.

2 Hold the flower nail between your thumb and index finger, then pipe an elongated arch that is narrower at the base and wider around the outer edge of the petal. Ensure that you start and finish piping at the same point and use a slightly damp paintbrush to tidy up the petal if necessary.

3 Lift the square of wax paper off the flower nail and rest the petal in a curved former or against a rolled up piece of kitchen paper to give the petal a gentle curve. Pipe several petals in slightly different sizes depending on how large you want the magnolia to be: I make approximately 12 petals for a magnolia. Leave them to dry for several hours.

4 When the petals are completely dry, peel away the wax paper and use a dusting brush to dust the narrow end of each petal with Soft Yellow dust food colour. Dust a thin, central line of Rose dust food colour about a ¼ of the way up the petal and remove any excess dust with an air puffer.

Note: This next step can either be done directly onto the cake or onto a larger piece of wax paper if you are preparing the magnolia ahead of time.

5 Select the best petals and arrange them on the work surface before you create the final flower. Colour a small amount of royal icing with Soft Yellow dust colour and stick the outer ring of petals in place with small bulbs of yellow icing. Make sure to leave enough space in the centre of the flower for the inner petals.

6 Stick down the next layer of petals inside the first ring in the same way. Once in place, support these inner petals with small pieces of kitchen paper or foam sponge to help them stand up as they dry. I have used six outer petals, three inner petals and then three central petals: the number of petals is a personal choice, but I have found that the more petals you add the heavier the magnolia looks. Leave the flower overnight to dry completely.

7 To create the flower centre, rub a little white vegetable fat on the end of a cocktail stick, then roll a small piece of Pale Yellow SFP into a

long teardrop shape. Insert the cocktail stick into the larger end of the teardrop and use pointed scissors to make small cuts into the paste and create a spiked cone. Leave the cone on the cocktail stick to firm for a few minutes, then dust it lightly with Rose dust food colour. Leave to dry overnight.

8 Colour a small amount of firm-peak royal icing with Cyclamen liquid colour, fit a silicone piping bag with a no. 1 piping nozzle then fill the bag ⅔ full with the pink icing. Make sure the cone is sitting loosely on the cocktail stick, then pipe small spikes around the base of the cone. Build up several layers of small spikes, then gently lift the cone off the cocktail stick by its tip, place it carefully in the centre of the magnolia and leave to dry. If you haven't made the magnolia directly on a cake, attach the flower once dry with a small bulb of royal icing.

tutor tip

If you're creating the magnolia on a piece of wax paper, make sure that each petal is attached to another otherwise the flower will not come off the paper in one piece.

magnificent magnolia

Simple and elegant, this magnificent magnolia cake would make the perfect gift for Mother's Day.

iced flowers

Magnolia, see pages 96 to 99

edibles

10cm (4") square cake, prepared for covering, see pages 17 to 21

20g (¾oz) SK Instant Mix Royal Icing

500g (1lb 1¾oz) SK Sugarpaste: Bridal White

SK Professional Paste Food Colour: Rose

100g (3½oz) SK Sugar Dough: Charcoal

Icing sugar in a shaker

SK Edible Glue

equipment

10cm (4") square thin cake board

15cm (6") square cake drum

Piping bag

Small palette knife

Small paintbrush

Double-sided tape

Satin ribbon (50mm width): burgundy

1 Prepare the cake for covering and place on a 10cm (4") square cake board. Colour the sugarpaste with a touch of Rose paste food colour and cover the cake with the pale pink sugarpaste (see pages 17 to 21).

2 Use the Rose paste colour to colour some more sugarpaste a darker shade of pink, then cover the cake drum with the dark pink paste. Secure the cake to the cake drum with a few bulbs of buttercream or royal icing.

3 Roll out some Charcoal Sugar Dough into a long strip approximately 41cm (16") long and 2.5cm (1") wide. Use a paintbrush with some edible glue to attach the grey paste as a ribbon around the base of the cake.

4 Attach the magnolia centrally on the top of the cake with a bulb of white royal icing. To finish, attach the burgundy ribbon around the cake drum with double-sided tape.

tulip pops

These tulip cake pops make pretty treats for a wedding, christening or party table and are a great idea for elegant edible favours.

edibles

Cake pop mixture (cake crumbs mixed with buttercream)

SK Instant Mix Royal Icing, approximately 20g (¾oz) per cake pop

SK Professional Liquid Food Colour: Rose

SK Easy Melt Choc Coating: White

SK Glycerine (optional)

equipment

SK 19cm (7½") Lollipop Sticks: Green

Microwaveable bowl

Piping bag

Piping nozzle: no. 104 (Wilton)

Small palette knife

Polystyrene block

Clear tape

Paintbrush

Air puffer (optional)

Scissors

Wide floristry ribbon: green

Template, see page 110

1 Make up a batch of cake pop mixture using your favourite recipe: I use approximately one part buttercream to three parts cake crumb. Roll the cake pop mixture into large teardrop shapes and then chill them in the refrigerator.

2 Melt the choc coating in a small, microwaveable bowl following the instructions on the packet. Dip the end of a lollipop stick into the melted coating and push the coated end of the stick into the wider end of the teardrop, pushing it in almost all the way to the tip. Repeat for each cake pop. Holding the stick, dip each cake pop into the melted white choc coating, then push the ends of the sticks into a polystyrene block and leave in the refrigerator to chill.

3 Make up some soft-peak royal icing and add glycerine to soften the icing when dry (see tip on page 106). Colour a small amount of the icing pink with Rose liquid food colour. Fit a piping bag with a no. 104 petal nozzle and place pale pink icing down the same side of the bag as the narrow end of the nozzle. Put white royal icing down the other side of the bag to make two-toned icing (see page 73). Using an arching motion, pipe three small overlapping petals at the very top

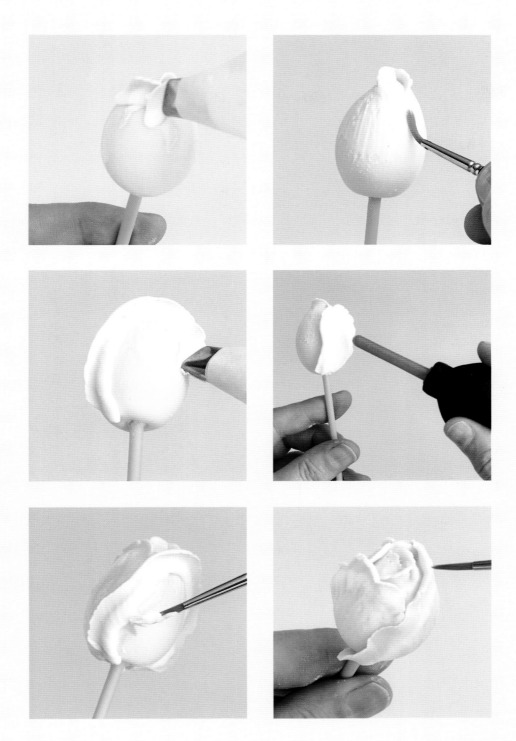

of the cake pop. Use a damp paintbrush to spread the icing from the bottom of the petals down the sides of the cake pop.

4 For the first large petal, start from the bottom of the cake pop and pipe up the side and over a join in two of the smaller petals, then back down the other side to the base. This is achieved more easily by turning both the cake pop and the nozzle at the same time: turn clockwise for right-handed pipers and anti-clockwise for left-handed pipers. Once you have piped the petal, use a damp paintbrush to smooth the icing down to the base of the cake pop but leave the outer edge of the petal untouched: this makes it look like the tulip petal has veins. Use an air puffer to encourage the sides of the petal to wrap around the cake pop.

5 Repeat step 4 to pipe the second petal so that it overlaps the first, but before you brush the icing down remove the edge of the previous petal with a damp paintbrush. Repeat for the third and final petal, but again remove the edges of the two overlapped petals before you brush the icing down to the base. Once the tulip is piped, use an air puffer to manipulate the edges of the petals to give them a more realistic appearance.

6 Using the template on page 110, cut a tulip leaf from a piece of wide green floristry ribbon. Position the leaf so that the tip is level with the top of the cake pop, and attach it to the cake pop stick with clear tape.

tutor tip

To make the royal icing softer and easier to eat for cake pops, cookies and cupcakes, add 1 teaspoon of glycerine to every 500g (1lb 1¾oz) of royal icing.

tutor tip

The majority of leaves can be piped in royal icing, buttercream or chocolate if they are piped directly onto the cake and are not likely to be disturbed during transit.

There is a variety of leaf nozzles on the market, however the two I find most useful are the no. 50 nozzle for miniature leaves and the no. 52 nozzle for average-sized leaves and larger. As royal icing leaves are not normally dusted, extra dimension can be added to them by making two shades of green icing. By filling one side of the piping bag with one shade and the opposite side with the other, you can pipe two-toned leaves for a more realistic finish. This works equally as well for piping a calyx onto the back of a rose or other flower.

A leaf nozzle has a larger V shaped notch on either side of its tip which will form the blades of the piped leaf. The smaller V shaped notch on the upper and lower sides of the tip will form the vein on the leaf.

piped leaves

edibles

SK Instant Mix Royal Icing

SK Professional Liquid Food Colours:
Holly/Ivy, Leaf Green or another green
colour of your choice

equipment

Piping bag (small)

Leaf nozzles: no. 50, 51 or 52
(depending on the size of the leaf
or calyx)

Piping nozzles: 1, 1.5 (PME)

Small palette knife

Fit a piping bag with a leaf nozzle then ²/₃ fill the bag with soft-peak green royal icing, two-toned if desired (see opposite).

Basic leaf: To make a basic leaf, rest the tip of the leaf nozzle on the surface of the cake where you wish the leaf to be placed and apply pressure to the piping bag. When the leaf has reached the required width, stop the pressure and gently pull the nozzle away from the end of the leaf: this will give you a sharp point if the royal icing is at the correct consistency.

Serrated leaf: To make a serrated leaf, rest the tip of the leaf nozzle on the surface of the cake where you wish the leaf to be placed. Apply pressure to the piping bag to start the leaf, then when it has reached the required width, gently move the tip of the nozzle in and out of the icing whilst elongating the leaf. To finish, stop the pressure and gently pull the nozzle away from the end of the leaf: this will give you a leaf similar to a single rose leaf.

Calyx: To create a calyx, follow the same method for the basic leaf and pipe five tiny leaves on the back of the flower: this can then be used to attach the flower to a cake.

templates

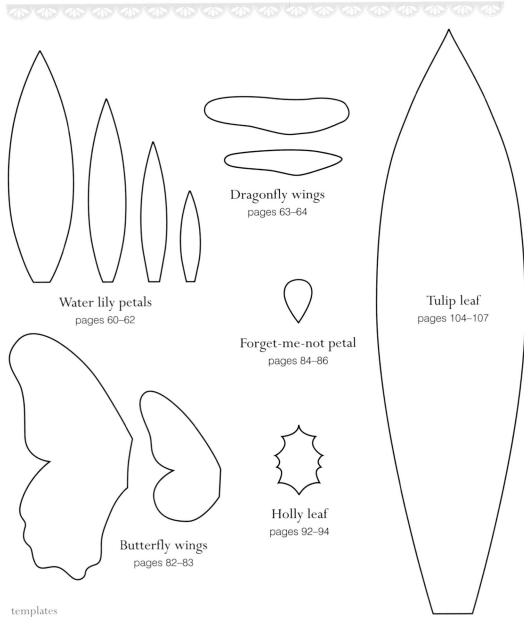

Water lily petals
pages 60–62

Dragonfly wings
pages 63–64

Forget-me-not petal
pages 84–86

Holly leaf
pages 92–94

Tulip leaf
pages 104–107

Butterfly wings
pages 82–83

suppliers

Squires Kitchen, UK
3 Waverley Lane
Farnham
Surrey
GU9 8BB
0845 61 71 810
+44 1252 260 260
www.squires-shop.com

Squires Kitchen
International School
The Grange
Hones Yard
Farnham
Surrey
GU9 8BB
0845 61 71 812
+44 1252 260262
www.squires-school.co.uk

Squires Kitchen, France
+33 (0) 1 82 88 01 66
clientele@squires-shop.fr
www.squires-shop.fr

Squires Kitchen, Italy
+44 (0) 1252 260 260
cliente@squires-shop.it
www.squires-shop.it

Squires Kitchen, Spain
+34 93 180 7382
cliente@squires-shop.es
www.squires-shop.es

SK Stockists

A Piece of Cake
Oxfordshire
www.sugaricing.com

Jane Asher Party Cakes
London
www.janeasher.com

Cake Craft World
Kent
www.cakecraftworld.co.uk

Design A Cake
Tyne & Wear
www.design-a-cake.co.uk

Surbiton Art & Sugarcraft
Surrey
www.surbitonart.co.uk

Windsor Cake Craft
Cheshire
www.windsorcakecraft.co.uk

SK Distributors, UK

Guy Paul & Co. Ltd.
Buckinghamshire
www.guypaul.co.uk

Culpitt Ltd.
Northumberland
www.culpitt.com

SK Distributors, Overseas

Russia

Dom Konditera
www.domkonditera.com

Sweden

Tårtdecor
Kungälv
www.tartdecor.se

Manufacturers

Smeg UK Ltd.
www.smeguk.com
www.smeg50style.co.uk

Italian appliance manufacturer
Smeg produces distinctive domestic
appliances combining design,
performance and quality.